# Conten

Published by Coordination Group Publications Ltd

*Contributors:* Taissa Csáky, Chris Dennett, Tim Major

ISBN: 978 1 84146 166 3
Groovy website: www.cgpbooks.co.uk
Jolly bits of clipart from CorelDRAW®

Printed by Elanders Hindson Ltd, Newcastle upon Tyne.

Text, design, layout and original illustrations © Coordination Group Publications Ltd. 2002

# Sneaky Words That Sound the Same

There are lots of words that <u>sound</u> the same,
but have <u>different spellings</u>.

*Learn these words so you don't get caught out.*

| | |
|---|---|
| no know | see sea |
| new knew | great grate |
| bow bough | I eye |
| be bee | in inn |
| right write | heard herd |
| threw through | might mite |
| hole whole | place plaice |
| are our | for four |

to two too

their there they're

you yew ewe

# *Adding* **s** *to Make Words Plural*

To make most words plural, just add **s**.

dog ➞ dog**s**    worm ➞ worm**s**    pill ➞ pill**s**

If the word ends in **h**, **s** or **x**, add **es**.

wis**h** ➞ wish**es**    brus**h** ➞ brush**es**

bu**s** ➞ bus**es**    glas**s** ➞ glass**es**

bo**x** ➞ box**es**    fo**x** ➞ fox**es**

For words that end with a <u>consonant</u> and **y**, take off **y** and add **ies**.

fl**y** ➞ fl**ies**    cit**y** ➞ cit**ies**

jel**ly** ➞ jel**lies**    ber**ry** ➞ ber**ries**

These plurals <u>don't</u> end in **s** — you have to <u>learn</u> them.

| teeth | mice | children |
| feet | deer | men |
| lice | fish | women |

# Making Words Ending in o or a Plural

To make most words ending in **o** and **a** plural, just add **s**.

armadill**o** ➝ armadill**os**        samos**a** ➝ samos**as**

igl**oo** ➝ iglo**os**        umbrell**a** ➝ umbrell**as**

pian**o** ➝ pian**os**        pizz**a** ➝ pizz**as**

cell**o** ➝ cell**os**        sof**a** ➝ sof**as**

You have to add **es** to <u>some</u> of the words that end in **o** to make them plural.

her**o** ➝ her**oes**        ech**o** ➝ ech**oes**

buffal**o** ➝ buffal**oes**        flaming**o** ➝ flaming**oes**

domin**o** ➝ domin**oes**        mang**o** ➝ mang**oes**

volcan**o** ➝ volcan**oes**        tornad**o** ➝ tornad**oes**

# Making Words Ending in **f** Plural

**Add S to any word ending in ff to make it plural.**

cuff ➞ cuffs          earmuff ➞ earmuffs

cliff ➞ cliffs          puff ➞ puffs

**Add es to a word ending in f or fe,
and change the f to a V.**

half ➞ halves          calf ➞ calves

loaf ➞ loaves          wolf ➞ wolves

scarf ➞ scarves          leaf ➞ leaves

shelf ➞ shelves          knife ➞ knives

thief ➞ thieves          wife ➞ wives

*LOOK OUT! These words break the rule — the f doesn't change.*

belief ➞ beliefs          chief ➞ chiefs

# Words With an 'OW' Sound

'OW' sounds can be spelt **ow**, or **ou**.

| ow | |
|---|---|
| h**ow** | **ow**l |
| c**ow** | h**ow**l |
| sh**ow**er | sc**ow**l |
| t**ow**el | gr**ow**l |
| f**ow**l | p**ow**er |

| ou | |
|---|---|
| **ou**t | f**ou**nd |
| sh**ou**t | p**ou**nd |
| h**ou**r | h**ou**nd |
| fl**ou**r | gr**ou**nd |

# Words With an 'OY' Sound

You can spell an 'OY' sound **oy**, or **oi**.

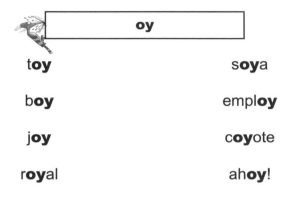

| oy | |
|---|---|
| t**oy** | s**oy**a |
| b**oy** | empl**oy** |
| j**oy** | c**oy**ote |
| r**oy**al | ah**oy**! |

| oi | |
|---|---|
| **oi**l | c**oi**n |
| b**oi**l | h**oi**st |
| f**oi**l | p**oi**nt |
| s**oi**l | p**oi**son |

If you're trying to spell a word with an 'oy' sound, think about whether you need **oy** or **oi**.

*Spelling Rules — Word Patterns*

# Words With an 'AIR' Sound

'AIR' sounds are spelt **air**, **ear**, **are** or **ere**.

| air | | ear | |
|---|---|---|---|
| h**air** | st**air**s | p**ear** | w**ear** |
| p**air** | **air**craft | b**ear** | t**ear** |

| are | | |
|---|---|---|
| c**are** | b**are** | fl**are**s |
| r**are** | h**are** | bew**are** |
| d**are** | sh**are** | nightm**are** |
| f**are** | sc**are** | squ**are** |

| ere | |
|---|---|
| wh**ere** | th**ere** |

# Words With an 'ER' Sound

You can spell an 'ER' sound **er**, **ir**, or **ur**.

| er | | | |
|---|---|---|---|
| h**er** | bigg**er** | h**er**d | hung**er** |
| tig**er** | long**er** | oth**er** | dang**er** |
| bak**er** | c**er**tain | p**er**son | beefburg**er** |

| ir |
|---|
| st**ir**    c**ir**cle |
| b**ir**d    d**ir**ty |
| g**ir**l    wh**ir**l |

| ur |
|---|
| p**ur**ple    t**ur**n |
| c**ur**ve    b**ur**n |
| c**ur**l    g**ur**gle |

*Spelling Rules — Word Patterns*

# Words With an 'OR' Sound

You can spell an 'OR' sound
**ore**, **aw**, **our**, **oor** or **au**.

| ore | | aw | |
|---|---|---|---|
| m**ore** | sc**ore** | s**aw** | str**aw** |
| s**ore** | ch**ore** | r**aw** | th**aw** |
| g**ore** | sh**ore** | p**aw** | colesl**aw** |
| c**ore** | bef**ore** | cl**aw** | jackd**aw** |

| our | | oor | |
|---|---|---|---|
| y**our**s | p**our** | d**oor** | p**oor** |
| f**our** | m**our**n | fl**oor** | m**oor** |

| au | |
|---|---|
| s**au**ce | **au**tumn |
| p**au**se | **au**ra |
| c**au**se | tr**au**ma |

# **qu** *Words*

Every time you write a **q**, follow it with a **u**.

| | |
|---|---|
| **qu**ick | **qu**estion |
| **qu**een | s**qu**eeze |
| **qu**iet | **qu**aver |
| **qu**ite | **qu**ay |
| **qu**ack | **qu**iver |
| **qu**ality | **qu**iz |
| **qu**antity | **qu**eue |
| **qu**arrel | **qu**it |
| **qu**arter | s**qu**id |
| s**qu**ash | **Qu**ebec |
| s**qu**are | **Qu**asimodo |

*Spelling Rules — Word Patterns*

# Words With **ce, ci** *or* **cy**

A **c** before an **e**, **i** or **y** <u>sounds like</u> an 's'.
<u>Don't forget</u> to use a **c** when you're writing these words.

| **ce** *words* | | | |
|---|---|---|---|
| **ce**real | **ce**lery | re**ce**ive | **ce**ntury |
| **ce**iling | re**ce**nt | des**ce**nd | **ce**ntigrade |
| De**ce**mber | **ce**ll | ex**ce**pt | **ce**ntipede |

| **ci** *words* | | | |
|---|---|---|---|
| **ci**rcle | **ci**ty | **ci**nema | de**ci**mal |
| **ci**rcus | **ci**tizen | **ci**nnamon | ac**ci**dent |
| **ci**rcuit | **ci**vil | in**ci**sor | dis**ci**pline |

| **cy** *words* | | | |
|---|---|---|---|
| fan**cy** | bi**cy**cle | **cy**linder | **cy**press |
| la**cy** | **cy**clist | mer**cy** | **cy**clone |

# Words With a **gh**

Spell the 'f' sound in these words **gh**.

tou**gh**    rou**gh**    enou**gh**    cou**gh**    trou**gh**

You can't hear the **gh** in these words.
Don't forget it when you're writing.

| ough | | ight | |
|---|---|---|---|
| dou**gh** | thou**gh**t | ei**gh**t | bri**gh**t |
| thou**gh** | bou**gh**t | li**gh**t | si**gh**t |
| thorou**gh** | brou**gh**t | mi**gh**t | ti**gh**t |
| throu**gh** | drou**gh**t | ri**gh**t | wei**gh**t |
| plou**gh** | sou**gh**t | fi**gh**t | frei**gh**t |
| bou**gh** | fou**gh**t | ni**gh**t | hei**gh**t |

*Spelling Rules — Word Patterns*

# ie *Words*

These words are all spelt with **ie**.

| | | |
|---|---|---|
| l**ie** | th**ie**f | p**ie**ce |
| p**ie** | br**ie**f | ch**ie**f |
| t**ie** | bel**ie**f | med**ie**val |
| fr**ie**d | f**ie**rce | pat**ie**nt |
| f**ie**ry | p**ie**rce | fr**ie**nd |
| f**ie**ld | pr**ie**st | misch**ie**f |
| sh**ie**ld | n**ie**ce | handkerch**ie**f |

5

# **ei** *Words*

These words are spelt with **ei**. You can tell because the **ei** sounds a bit like capital 'A'.

**ei**ght    r**ei**ns    v**ei**l    r**ei**gn

w**ei**gh    v**ei**n    fr**ei**ght    n**ei**ghbour

After **c** you nearly always put **ei**.

re**cei**ve    re**cei**pt    **cei**ling    de**cei**ve

*A few words break the rule.*

s**cie**nce    gla**cie**r    an**cie**nt

These **ei** words don't follow a rule, so you just have to <u>learn them</u>.

**ei**ther    th**ei**r    prot**ei**n    for**ei**gn

n**ei**ther    w**ei**rd    h**ei**ght    sover**ei**gn

*Spelling Rules — Word Patterns*

# Silent **k** and Silent **g**

These words all start with a **k**.
<u>Don't forget</u> the **k** when you write them down.

| | | |
|---|---|---|
| **k**now | **k**nob | **k**nuckle |
| **k**not | **k**nife | **k**nit |
| **k**nee | **k**nock | **k**nickers |
| **k**neel | **k**night | |

*<u>Don't</u> say the **k** out loud when you're reading.*

These words all start with a **g**.
<u>Don't forget</u> the **g** when you write them down.

*<u>Don't</u> say the **g** out loud when you're reading.*

| | |
|---|---|
| **g**naw | **g**nashed |
| **g**nat | **g**narled |
| **g**nu | **g**nomes |

# *Silent l and Silent h*

These words all have a silent **l**.
<u>Don't forget</u> the **l** when you write them down.

| | | |
|---|---|---|
| ha**l**f | yo**l**k | wou**l**d |
| ca**l**m | fo**l**k | cou**l**d |
| cha**l**k | sa**l**mon | shou**l**d |
| ca**l**f | | |

*<u>Don't</u> say the **l** out loud when you're reading.*

These words all have a silent **h**.
<u>Don't forget</u> the **h** when you write them down.

| | | |
|---|---|---|
| w**h**ere | w**h**eat | c**h**emist |
| w**h**en | w**h**ale | r**h**ubarb |
| w**h**at | w**h**ine | r**h**yme |
| w**h**irl | | r**h**ino |

*<u>Don't</u> say the **h** out loud when you're reading.*

*Spelling Rules — Silent Letters*

# Silent **w** and Silent **b**

These words all have a silent **W**.
Don't forget the **W** when you write them down.

| | | |
|---|---|---|
| **w**rite | **w**rist | **w**rapper |
| **w**rong | **w**rinkle | **w**retch |
| ans**w**er | s**w**ord | **w**restle |
| **w**reck | | **w**rangler |

*Don't say the **w** out loud when you're reading.*

These words all have a silent **b**.
Don't forget the **b** when you write them down.

| | | |
|---|---|---|
| lam**b** | tom**b** | de**b**t |
| num**b** | bom**b** | dou**b**t |
| dum**b** | crum**b** | su**b**tle |
| thum**b** | plum**b** | |

*Don't say the **b** out loud when you're reading.*

# Letters That Are Hard to Hear

When you <u>say</u> these words, you <u>can't hear</u> all the letters properly. <u>Learn</u> the spellings <u>now</u> so you get them right.

We**d**nesday        autum**n**        gover**n**ment        cent**re**

| a |
|---|

diction**a**ry        station**a**ry

libr**a**ry        prim**a**ry

| i |
|---|

bus**i**ness        eas**i**ly

fam**i**ly        def**i**nite

| e |
|---|

gen**e**ral        station**e**ry

diff**e**rent        fright**e**ning

int**e**resting        jewell**e**ry

| o |
|---|

fact**o**ry        categ**o**ry

pois**o**nous        cath**o**lic

mem**o**rable        explanat**o**ry

*These words are made by joining two words. When you're writing, say the two words separately in your head — it will help you remember all the letters.*

gran**d**mother        han**d**kerchief        ras**p**berry

win**d**mill        han**d**bag        cu**p**board

# Words Ending With **ing**

To make <u>most words</u> end with **ing**, just add **ing**.

| | | |
|---|---|---|
| do**ing** | pull**ing** | meet**ing** |
| walk**ing** | push**ing** | tick**ing** |
| talk**ing** | say**ing** | paint**ing** |
| sing**ing** | read**ing** | guard**ing** |

If there's an **e**, <u>take it off</u> before you add **ing**.

writ**e** ➝ writ**ing**

tak**e** ➝ tak**ing**

mak**e** ➝ mak**ing**

star**e** ➝ star**ing**

smil**e** ➝ smil**ing**

amaz**e** ➝ amaz**ing**

decid**e** ➝ decid**ing**

# Words Ending With **ing**

When you add **ing**, <u>double</u> the <u>last letter</u> of a word if it comes <u>straight after</u> a short vowel.

*A <u>short vowel</u> is one that makes a short sound.*
*e.g. The 'a' in* **plan** *is <u>short</u>, but the 'a' in* **plane** *is long.*

si**t** ➞ si**tt**ing

ru**n** ➞ ru**nn**ing

ho**p** ➞ ho**pp**ing

shu**t** ➞ shu**tt**ing

cla**p** ➞ cla**pp**ing

sho**p** ➞ sho**pp**ing

cha**t** ➞ cha**tt**ing

pla**n** ➞ pla**nn**ing

ti**p** ➞ ti**pp**ing

be**t** ➞ be**tt**ing

wi**n** ➞ wi**nn**ing

# Changing **y** to **i**

Change **y** at the <u>end</u> of a word into **i** when you <u>add</u> letters.

### Adding **er**

funn**y** ⟶ funn**i**er

craz**y** ⟶ craz**i**er

luck**y** ⟶ luck**i**er

### Adding **est**

happ**y** ⟶ happ**i**est

chill**y** ⟶ chill**i**est

runn**y** ⟶ runn**i**est

### Adding **ed**

fr**y** ⟶ fr**i**ed

sp**y** ⟶ sp**i**ed

marr**y** ⟶ marr**i**ed

carr**y** ⟶ carr**i**ed

### Adding **es**

cr**y** ⟶ cr**i**es

rel**y** ⟶ rel**i**es

tr**y** ⟶ tr**i**es

hurr**y** ⟶ hurr**i**es

### Adding **ness**

dirt**y** ⟶ dirt**i**ness

laz**y** ⟶ laz**i**ness

wind**y** ⟶ wind**i**ness

empt**y** ⟶ empt**i**ness

### Adding **ly**

happ**y** ⟶ happ**i**ly

prett**y** ⟶ prett**i**ly

heav**y** ⟶ heav**i**ly

read**y** ⟶ read**i**ly

# Words Ending With **ful**

There are <u>no</u> words ending in 'full'. Always use **ful**.

hand**ful**     pain**ful**     wonder**ful**

mouth**ful**     hope**ful**     colour**ful**

play**ful**     care**ful**     harm**ful**

fear**ful**     wake**ful**     faith**ful**     thank**ful**

doubt**ful**     scorn**ful**     fear**ful**     boast**ful**

Turn **y** at the <u>end</u> of a word into **i** when you <u>add</u> **ful**.

beaut**y** ⟶ beaut**iful**

plent**y** ⟶ plent**iful**

fanc**y** ⟶ fanc**iful**

merc**y** ⟶ merc**iful**

pit**y** ⟶ pit**iful**

# Words Ending With **ic**

com**ic**          mag**ic**

mus**ic**          angel**ic**

man**ic**          rhythm**ic**

traff**ic**          energet**ic**

scientif**ic**          metall**ic**

atom**ic**          acid**ic**

epidem**ic**          superson**ic**

Remove the **y** at the <u>end</u> of a word when you <u>add</u> **ic**.

histor**y** ➞ histor**ic**          horrif**y** ➞ horrif**ic**

allerg**y** ➞ allerg**ic**          terrif**y** ➞ terrif**ic**

photograph**y** ➞ photograph**ic**

# Words Ending With **i,** **u,** and **v**

There are hardly any words that end in **i**, **u**, or **v**.

### Words ending in **i**

mini

taxi

### Words ending in **u**

gnu

guru

### Words ending in **v**

shiv — A shiv *is a kind of knife.*

spiv — A spiv *is a crook.*

If you write a word ending with **i**, **u**, or **v**, <u>stop</u> and <u>think</u>. You might have left off an **e**.

| | | |
|---|---|---|
| lov**e** | blu**e** | eeri**e** |
| liv**e** | rescu**e** | avenu**e** |
| wav**e** | tissu**e** | geni**e** |

# Words Ending With **le,** **el** *and* **al**

The word endings **le**, **el** and **al**, all <u>sound</u> the same.
You've got to <u>learn</u> the ending for each word.

## le

| | | |
|---|---|---|
| tab**le** | midd**le** | unc**le** |
| litt**le** | app**le** | circ**le** |
| marb**le** | kett**le** | bicyc**le** |
| tick**le** | bubb**le** | cand**le** |
| pick**le** | pudd**le** | need**le** |
| chuck**le** | wobb**le** | pood**le** |

## el

parc**el**

mod**el**

tunn**el**

## al

met**al**

magic**al**

practic**al**

# Words Ending With **ible** *and* **able**

## These words all end with **ible**.

| | |
|---|---|
| horr**ible** | invinc**ible** |
| terr**ible** | ed**ible** |
| respons**ible** | revers**ible** |
| poss**ible** | sens**ible** |
| incred**ible** | indestruct**ible** |

## These words all end with **able**.

| | |
|---|---|
| **able** | miser**able** |
| reli**able** | envi**able** |
| enjoy**able** | break**able** |
| prob**able** | respect**able** |
| valu**able** | dispos**able** |
| ador**able** | agree**able** |

**ible** *and* **able** *endings sound just the same. Learn these words so you <u>know</u> which to use.*

*Spelling Rules — Word Endings*

# Words Ending With **tion** *and* **ian**

The last bit of these words sounds like 'shun', but you spell it **tion**.

| | | |
|---|---|---|
| lo**tion** | atten**tion** | conserva**tion** |
| fic**tion** | punctua**tion** | educa**tion** |
| direc**tion** | correc**tion** | communica**tion** |
| mo**tion** | pronuncia**tion** | posi**tion** |
| frac**tion** | pollu**tion** | construc**tion** |
| subtrac**tion** | vibra**tion** | revolu**tion** |

Words about where people or things come from usually end in **ian**, not 'ion'.

| | |
|---|---|
| Russ**ian** | Mart**ian** |
| Venet**ian** | Croat**ian** |

ERS21